Epic Philosophies in
Love, War, & Reasoning Vol. 2:

Hidden Glory

By
Thomas S. Doland

Dedicated to my mother, Ida.

TABLE OF CONTENTS

Preface 1

Introduction...2

Rain 4

Same Book Another Page 6

Remembering the words 7

Solace 9

Coming Togethers...10

Consideration 11

Lied To Me...13

Please Do Tell...15

One Day 16

Riding Out The Storm 18

Journeyman..20

Ship Of Dreams 22

The Call..23

End Of The Highway 24

Tightrope 25

Fast Lane...26

Too Dark To See..27

No Strangers...28

Caught Up In A Maze 29

Saturday..31

Walk Away 33

Another Day 34

Cocoon...36

Erase The Stain...37

Test Of Time...38

Surrender All..39

Shelter..40

Searching..41

Satisfaction...43

My Strength..50

Hidden Glory...47

Clear Skies..49

Glory..50

None of the tears..52

Not Just A Feeling...53

Every Tear...55

Path In The Sky..57

No Matter How Far..58

South Wind Blows...60

Polished Shoes...61

Promise..63

Whirlwind..64

All Along..66

Mark Of A Man..67

Seasons..69

Spirit Wind..72

About The Author...74

Preface

Traveling the world's nations and cultures breaks the mold of encapsulated thinking. It opens human suffering and passion. Societies torn by culture wars worldwide reveal the tenderness of the human drama. From towers of power dynasties to hidden slave camps, the orphans of compassion seek asylum.

Mysteries of culture hidden by colorful tradition hide the trauma of caste systems. Heartless governments uprooting families into endless migration to nowhere. Highways of broken dreams and lives seeking hope for new life and fulfillment. These works capture the essence of the ocean's tides and waves of love, desire, passion, and vision.

Let your imagination relocate you to another world. Perhaps the refueling of your own existence. Welcome to the travels into your heart and soul.

Introduction

Man's intellect and education have not put his best foot forward. In this poetic and lyrical journey, we take another heartfelt visual ride on the rocky roads of the human journey.

Though sophisticated, some cultures may like to think of themselves, they have provided no assurance of a peaceful existence with the necessary ingredients to live healthy and free.

It's a grand illusion provided by city lights. While under their Illumination is the sad reality of racism, injustice, violence, and corruption. Not only to humanity, his brothers and sisters, but also to the earth, the mothers. Will this all fall into a cataclysmic disaster, or will there be a rising to the occasion to resurrect a new era of reconstruction of wellbeing and humanitarian dignity. This volume is another exciting and challenging read. Hidden Glory. Enjoy. Ponder. Bring resolution

Rain

I walk through this world
That's so full of hurt
With faces so full of pain
Wondering how can it go on
When will it end
Lord send us the rain

Hearts that are broken
Words full of hate
How long can it endure
The clock's running out
How will they make out
Lord send us the rain

The ground is hard and cracked
The pressure is breaking through
Life agonizing the light of day
The price of pleasure
Is showing its face
Lord send us the rain

Send us your promise
Send your mercy and grace
Send us fresh water again
We thirst for your presence
Like the deer at the brook
Lord send us the rain

Same Book Another Page

Can't run away from words
They will surely find their mark
Their destiny has been determined
The center of your heart

Shot like arrows
In a fearsome rage
Caught in a crossfire
Same book another page

Look for a door
Must be an escape
Hard to hide a heart
When it's in tender shape

Don't want to retaliate
That's not really me
Just want to talk it out
Supposed to be friends
You see

To be someone else
I just can't really be
I've spent enough time
Just trying to be me

Remembering the words
Of the seasoned sage
Like the winds across the desert
From another age
Caught in the crossfire
Same book another page

When the smoke has cleared
Supposedly you walk away
Like nothing's been done
What's there left to say
Only a heart left undone

Just like a curtain
Pulled on a stage
Same book another page

Fight back the fears
That assaults your very dreams
Fight back the tears
The heart beached like a ship
By the oceans streams

Must find someone
To rescue my heart
Perhaps a friend will come
I feel taken apart

That was yesterday
Life must go on
There are many tomorrows
Another play of the pawn

Life must get easier
As years bring on age
Caught in the crossfire
Same book another page

Solace

Oh that my soul was satisfied
In your presence
Oh that I would not faint
In the desert of faded dreams
Oh that they would not be
Blown away like the sands
In the desert wind
Oh that hope would stir
And awaken my heart
Oh that your light
Would press into the darkness
And chase away the shadows
Oh my strength and song
Return to me
As the dawn dew
that I would again
Find the joy
And wellspring
Of your delight
Save me
I am dwelling
In a desert place

Coming Together

Of everything you contemplate
What do you find
Have great ideas
Plans and dreams

All is coming together
In your great scheme
Of all you are thinking
What did you find

The parts and pieces
Coming together
Sealed with a frayed tether
Filling your mind

All this held in one grand place
the center of your mind
Years of building a case
What did you find

You put your hand to a vapor
A whisper in your mind
Helping no one
But yourself

You helped not a soul
The future you hold
Is all in your head

Consideration

Missed opportunities
Still cross my mind
Would life be the same
If I had taken the time
To seriously consider
Decisions and choices
And destiny's call

Missed opportunities
Make you think back
How the power of choice
Makes up each path
It's hard to believe
For the most part it's true
The future you hold
Is determined mostly by you

Would life be different
Perhaps maybe better
Perhaps maybe worse
Choices circumstances
Can't be rehearsed

Had the conscience
Been the compass
Had emotions not
Had their say
Would one have seen ahead
To avoid difficulty today

No promise exists
At life would be kind
No guarantee
Of a silver spoon and wine
Only wisdom can lend
Its voice to the part
The discipline of decisions
The weighing of the heart

A future is tuned
To destiny's march
How careful then
Should decisions be made
Would pondering the choices
Make any difference at all
Standing on the fault line
Of destiny's call

Lied To Me

The city lights are bright
When you are just a child
The innocence of a heart
That hasn't been defiled
The pathway seems so golden
The future seems so sure
The world is a treasure chest
To try it all is the lure
The pleasure of music
It seems will never end
The nights full of possibility
So do it all while you can
When you have gotten as high
As you think you can go
When they are selling you more
But there is nothing to show
When you have sold out your soul
To the highest bid
Your hearts worn out
You've only yourself to kid
They lied to you
Gone as far as they could

The lights led to darkness
Only the wise knew they would
They lied to me
Said that their way was right
But the farther I went
Was deeper into the night
They lied to me
They lied to you
Jesus is the only way
He will forever be true
Don't follow the lights
The brightness of this world
They will bring you to nothing
Of this you can be sure
The pathway is wide
That leads to death
But the narrow way to Jesus
Will bring you rest
They lied to me
They lied to you
Now is the time
To trust Him that is true

Please Do Tell

Please tell me you are happy
The way things are in life
Is this what you were born for
From birth until you meet the night

Tell me you are at peace
Things that are in the news
Does it matter things go bad to worse
Is that ok with you

Show me you are satisfied
That all is going so well
Ignore what you don't believe is true
That life is perfect in your little shell

Tell me you are fulfilled
Working out life numb and blind
You are only here for a short while
Does this complete your little time

Please tell me you are unaware
That your life is just like smoke
You drift through a few short years
Hoping that this all was not a joke

Please tell me there is a heaven
You know there is a hell
Does it make you any difference
Please do tell

One Day

One day this old dam is gonna break
One day this old dam is gonna break
She's just made of sticks and stones
She's been strong but not for long
One day this old dam is gonna break

One day this old dam is gonna break
One day this old dam is gonna break
Rain just keeps a fallin'
Waters deepern I ever saw it
One day this old dam is gonna break

I've seen this day acomin'
Will be too late for runnin'
One day this old dam is gonna break

One day this old dam is gonna break
One day this old dam is gonna break
Better get your hat and shoes on
Looks like it won't be long

One day this old dam is gonna break

Riding Out The Storm

I see the storm clouds gatherin’
The wind and sea are still
The sails are up the rudder set
The watchman’s cry is shrill

The winds they are a comin’
Waves must be twenty feet high
Set the ship into the breeze
The storm is comin’ nigh

The waves are crashing on the deck
The mainsails lash is torn
I hope the ship holds through the night
To see tomorrow morn’

The ship must be secured
The ship’s cargo is thrown overboard
The storm must be endured
It blows for days and many nights

Our strength is failin’ fast
Unless the hand of God prevails
We fear we will not last

The alarm is sounded, land is near
The anchors must be dropped
We must not crash into the shore
Our headway must be stopped

The hand of God must show the way
Through life's stormy seas
We don't know all the ways and means
As we travel in the breeze

We must put weights and cares aside
To make it to the goal
We don't always understand
As we near the rocks and shoals
But we put ourselves into His hands
Out of our own control
To make it through another test
His way and not our own

Journeyman

In this journey of life
There's a pathway of light
That leads up to heaven's door
Only you can decide
Only you can choose
When you come
To the fork in the road
It's a choice of the heart
But you've known from the start
The way
That will lead you home

The long winding path
Makes a way of its own
Following an uncharted course
It's a pathway to life
To those who search hard
Only you can secure the way
The journey of decisions
Another stone in the path
You walk it deep in your heart

It's like the call of the sea
With the sound of its waves
It's salt spray scent in the air
Calls the journeyman to discover
It's expanse and depth
To find its unsearchable ways

The heart hears the calling
It follows the way
Searching beyond the soul
It's a choice of the heart
The heart hears the calling
It follows the way
Searching beyond the soul
It's a choice of the heart

You've known from the start
The way
That will
Take you home

Ship Of Dreams

No place for thoughts
No place for means
No place for ideas
No place for esteem

Kicked off the ship
Of dreams in midstream
Hole of hopelessness
Place of no means

Crawled up on the beach
The ship was gone
Fell asleep in the sand
I was unknown

No place for thoughts
No place for dreams
No place for ideas
No place for esteem

Kicked off the ship
Of dreams in midstream
Sucked by a maelstrom
To the place of no means

The Call

Voices call across the desert
Voices call across the sea
Wasted lives
Are they no reason
Can you hear the cries and plea's
Hungry hearts in a desperate season
Trembling hearts full of pain
Can their cry reach inside you
Have you shut them out
Again
Fainting cries within the prison
Breaking hearts line the streets
Is your heart too contented
Can't stop to give relief
Do you turn your eyes away
From the desperate vacant stare
Do you still hide your heart away
Or just too busy to even care

End Of The Highway

Riding these old highways
Till there is no more place
Looking everywhere for freedom
Have to find an escape

Gone to the ends of the highways
To find peace of mind
It would only be fair to tell you
There is nothing there to find

Surrounded by confusion
Everyone seems to know
All of them have conflicting answers
Twisting and turning as they go

Everyone pointing fingers
That's the way to go
I find it still amazing
They all say that they know

Concepts to conclusions
The strong push the hungry away
There is no place to go
Where someone does not pay

Every dark alley to the halls of fame
The twists and turns of fate
They all have your name
All that is left
Is posting an arrival date

Tightrope

Are you walking the line
Can't tell right from wrong
Just playing the field
To whatever is in sight

Off to the right
Off to the left
There's nothing to convince you
You're on the pathway
To death

It seems so convenient
To do anything you want
But the life of the heart
Is only a haunt

Walking the tightrope
It's all just in fun
Walking the tightrope
There's nothing left undone

Walking the tightrope
It's a highway to hell'
Walking the tightrope
Nothing's left to tell

Fast Lane

On a ride in the fast lane
Passing up exits one by one
It's too much of a thrill
To slow down now
You are having too much fun

On a fast ride past midnight
Lane markers turn to lines
The radio is sounding mellow
Everything is feeling fine

Suddenly there are tail lights
A flatbed windshield high
Coming too fast to avoid it
Too late for any good bye

Your future is very questionable
You've lost your self-respect
Unless you cry to Jesus
There is little you can expect

Riding in the first lane
You will certainly end up a wreck

Too Dark To See

On the highway of time to come
Looked back on the road
Where I came from
On this highway of time
My sight has grown dim

To this highway of time
I have succumb
Looking back the sun has set
On time long gone by
Looking forward to the rising sun

Too bright for my eyes to see
Perhaps I don't want to know
What's ahead for me
On the highway of time to come

There are no strangers
To the highway of time
Just casualties of traveling alone
Day dawns with a great sigh
Day ends with a final done

No Strangers

On the highway of time to come
I looked back on the road
From time I was from
On the highway of time
I have succumb

Looking back the sun sets
On time long gone by
Looking forward the sun rises
Too bright for my eyes

Perhaps I don't want to see
What's ahead for me
On the highway of time to come

There are no strangers
To the highway of time
As many as there are
They all travel along

The day dawns with a great sigh
The sun sets with a final goodbye
They all travel along

Caught Up In A Maze

Life lost in the shuffle
Of times quickening pace
At a loss for direction
Caught up in a maze
No time for rhyme or reason
It's only what's at hand
Life is drained at days end
And you still can't understand

When the lights are out
And you're there all alone
There's no one there to boast
The dread of thought
To glimpse inside
And realize life's
Fragile's post

The search for fulfillment
And a meaningful task
Pull daily at the heart of desire

But the hand pulls back
An empty glass
Life's fire
Is slowly quenched
The call has been clear
Time and again

A beckon to come home
Release the hold of earthly desire
You have never really been alone
Most times we take for granted
The ways and means for man
But in that secret hiding place
Of God
He has the perfect plan
It only stands to reason
He desires to show the way
He created man to be like Him
And walk in that light each day
When lights are out
All alone
Your heart cries out for peace
With the heart and soul
Laid open to God
He will touch you
And loneliness will cease

Saturday

It was Saturday
You took the time away
From following the way
You know is right
Now it's Tuesday
It's time to pay
There's no peace of mind
In sight
It was easy
For the moment
Now guilt has its
Blinding hold
No going back
The bridge is crossed
A guilty conscience
Will take its toll
Didn't remember
The price you paid
The last time
You followed your soul
It's a hard way
It's a hard day
To wander away
From the Lord
It's a cold heart
It was a good start

The world took its
Stranglehold
There's one way out
There's one way in
It's escaping the grip of sin
But Love reigns
He can heal the pain
Come running
Back to his love
Love reigns
He can set you free
Love reigns
It's so plain to see
You are a long long way
From home

Walk Away

It's just another Monday
Life is on fast pace
Minding the priorities
Competing in the race
It's business just as usual
Meeting daily foes
Having victory as the hours pass
Staying on your toes

Without particular warning
The temptation button is pushed
It sends your mind reeling
Common sense is just about hushed
The pulse rate starts racing
Decision time is here
Will this be another victory
or posting for another fear

Righteousness is living
By Christ in you today
Post another victory to the blood
Turn around and walk away

Another Day

How long is a day
How long is a night
Can loneliness be stayed
Can wrong be made right

Abandoned by trusting
Circumstance reveals
True heart's feelings
When betrayal is near

Fair weather friends
Are close when you're right
Who can find a friend
Walking alone in the night

Abandoned by the one
Who carried me in the womb
Streetlights are a friend
When you're alone in the night

Who will break the darkness
To find the wandering life
Are they worth the time
Just leave to their own demise

Only the soul
Penetrated by heaven's light
Has seeing eyes
Can hear the cry
In the darkness

Compassion to befriend
the wonderer
And bring the loneliness
To an end

Cocoon

I've decided to go to heaven
Too much trouble in this place
The idea things are going well
Is just about erased
Nothing getting better
But getting worse
The world has deepened
Its dark embrace
A cocoon is the only escape

Monster blindness has men subdued
They have no heart to feel
Good is despised only to
Wait for the open recipient hell
Only a few have the light to see
A facsimile is in place
Souls stolen away in a deceptive heist
The martyrs have won their race

I've decided to go to heaven
Too much trouble in this place
There remains much work to do
It's a very dangerous race

Erase The Stain

Not my way
My life is not my own
Not today
Living life all alone

It's not my plan that you see
It's all written in destiny
It's directly from the heart of God
A plan to make me completely free

Not your way
Life can't be the same
Not today
Living life in the rain

It's not your plan that you see
Your life can be made completely free
The plan is directly from above
Straight from the heart of life and love

It's completely up to you my friend
To have a Life that never ends
You can escape the pouring rain
Have Jesus erase the deep dark stain

So open up your hardened heart
Today you have a brand new start
You'll soon see it's the only way
To live life freely every day

Test Of Time

There is no escaping the heartache
There is no escaping the pain
There is no running from disappointment
There is no avoiding the rain

The clouds do not seem to go away
There does not seem reason or rhyme
Just be faithful to God all through it
Just standing the test of time

It is hard to understand it
It does not seem just or due
If you give your best
To stand the test
The pure in heart will make it through

Walking away would be easy
Turning back would seem okay
It is all in your power
To keep your heart true
The faithful will see the way

Surrender All

When will the heart surrender
Captive feelings of doubt and fear
Reminding the soul of memories
That holds a future unclear

Opportunities passed on the roadside
Ideas blown away in the wind
A heart that sways with the stormy seas
Surging tides that never end

All hope grows near the rivers
God's pure deep healing streams
It flows from deep inside that city
From under the heavenly scenes

From the depths of His compassion
The angels and the Spirit of God
Are dispatched with power to set free
By His Name, His Promise and His Word

Chains of torment are broken
Darkness of doubt subdued
Faith marks another victory
The Resurrected Testimony
On the throne of God prevails

Shelter

One day I was happy
One day I was sad
One day I was laughing
Next day I was mad
Balance was illusive
Grip was not to be found
Echoes from all directions
Slippery surfaces all around
No rhyme or reason for anything
My conscience screaming foul
Got to find an exit
Got to find a grip right now
Got to find some shelter
A way out of this mess
A friend nowhere to be found
It was midnight
My soul cried out
God I can't make it another day
Soaked in sweat
Down on my knees
Help came from heaven
Years of captivity broken
Heart and soul set free

Searching

They're searching
You're searching
We're searching
For someone to love us

They're searching
You're searching
We're searching
Looking for a better way

Every day
Get longer and longer

God's love keeps drawing
Stronger and stronger

He will free you
He will keep you
Show you a better way

Keep crying
Keep trying
You'll feel
His touch on your heart

He will draw you
He will keep you
He will never depart

So keep searching
Keep searching
You will find His
Better way

So keep searching
Keep on searching

Satisfaction

It's one of life's greatest tragedies
To be what you have never been inclined
Living life after others' opinions
It's a future with a bad design

Everyone saying this or that
The heavy overhead
Never paying attention
That it never seemed to fit
It's a pattern that leaves
True dreams dead

Being pressed into a certain figure
Someone you were never meant to be
No wonder you have been so uncertain
From far away it's easy to see

Is it no wonder there is such dissatisfaction
Is it no wonder life feels so bare
It finally comes to the point you say
I really just don't care

A thought can change your destiny
It can pull you out of a rut
There has been a right way all along
Others' opinions must be cut

It's really a cultivation process
To some it comes naturally
To others a lifetime struggle
Sinking into opinions sea

The plan can be uncovered
Like mining for a vein of gold
Pulling years of dirt and rock away
The dream is yet to unfold

Is it no wonder there is so much dissatisfaction
Is it no wonder life becomes a bore
It finally comes to the point you say
I've got to get to the core

It's a long and lengthy process
Much patience brought to bear
But as far as others' opinions go
I just don't really care

Always living to please others
Never possessing what's really you
I suppose it could be an honest mistake
Until the truth comes into view

Some like putting others into classes
It makes them feel secure
They will always put you below them
Such thinking is so impure

So away with others' opinions
Your future and dreams are at stake
God has had a plan from the beginning
It's yours the next move to make

There is a place of satisfaction
The plan God surely will share
But as far as others' opinions go
I just don't really care

So hearing hear
And search for truth
Results will surely come to bear

But for just anyone's opinion
I just don't really care

My Strength

When will it be over
When will the struggle end
My race is just beginning
On Him I must depend

He took me from a deep dark pit
And clothed me with His light
He set me on my feet to run
And said now you must learn to fight

It seems when I'm my weakest
He calls on me to stand
He holds me up to take the test
And says son I understand

He's laid a path before me
Sometimes the struggle is fierce
But I hope in hope to see His face
And hold the hands once pierced

O my Lord and my God
Strengthen me today
I make my stand before the world
I'll follow you in Your way

Hidden Glory

The morning sun glares across
The thirsty plain
And chases the dawn shadows
Darkness flees to far corners
Another cloudless day arrives
The brown parched grass
Stretches forever
Until it touches the horizon sky
A lone eagle soars in the
Wind currents
Searching for prey
Even a carcass will satisfy
Perhaps under the dried branches
Of a scrub tree
Life fleeting in hopeless wait
For rain

The wind blows through the grass
To and fro
Like invisible fingers working
An uncharted course
A small herd of deer
Graze the dried range
A stream bed empty and cracked
Keeps them near
In hope of it being filled
Once again

Nature itself pleads
For early rain
That it may refresh the root and stalk
Once again bringing life
Leaves and fruit
The morning sun follows the trek
Along its destined path
Clouds appear on the distant horizon
Moving as guided by the will of an
Invisible force toward the stricken
Plain

Hope is mounted up as the wind
Is filled with the scent of rain
The deer leap as in rejoicing
As the clouds release their bounty
The stream is filled
The wind celebrates
The falling rain
Sending the eagle into new heights
Scrub tree branches crackle together
In the wind as if clapping
The grass bows in honor
Its plea heard in the heavens
Revealing its hidden glory

Clear Skies

You hear a distant thunder
Here comes the rain again
I hope it's not a bad storm
It's coming from clouds within
There's such a great expectation
A certain pressure to perform
How do you just be yourself
And find shelter from the storm

Is it a feeling of not being accepted
Do you not fit into the form
How do you get free
From feeling incomplete
It's not just running from the storm

You just start feeling confident
There's been a healing stream
But when you reach to touch it
It seems to be just a dream

You know that there is a purpose
But it seems so far away
Deep down inside you feel it
You just settle for being okay

Look expectantly
Beyond these earthly skies
The clouds will be swept away
Jesus will come tenderly
And wipe the fears away

Glory

You say you want to walk in His righteousness
You say you want to walk in His love
You say you want to walk like the Son of God
Take hold of the gift from above

You say you want more of His holiness
You say you want to walk by His side
You say you want to walk like a Son of God
You've got to let go of the pride

Walking in his holy presence
Taking up his majestic life
You can't hold on to selfishness
You're going to have to lose your life

I feel His holy presence
Taking hold of my life once again
His blood cleansed my inner chamber
His glory is flooding in

None of the Tears

None of the tears
Have passed me by
None of the fears
Have let me by

None of the sorrow let me be
Come sweet Jesus set me free

Years of pain
Left my heart so weak
Years of loneliness
Left my soul in sleep

None of the sorrow let me be
Come sweet Jesus set me free

What heart can trust
When its cords are broken
What heart can mend
When hard words are spoken

The weary traveler must find his way
The life with no purpose the price to pay
How many years will you let pass by
Let my sweet Jesus
Wipe the tears from your eyes

Not Just A Feeling

You're always looking
For someone to talk to
You're always looking
For someone to care
All that you need
Is to look to Jesus
He's always waiting
He's always there
It's a fine thing
To find someone to talk to
A gesture quite friendly
A heart made to share
All that you need
Is a heart filled with Jesus
A quick look around
And He's standing right there

Just listen close
And you will hear Him calling
Just listen close
He's calling your name
It's not just a feeling
He's looking to give you
It's all that He is
And you're never the same
No need to go
Far away searching

No need to go looking
For someone to care
Just look to Jesus
He's all that you're needing
Just turn around
He'll be right there

Every Tear

Every tear that you've cried
He knows the hurt
That you feel inside

Every tear when you're alone
He knows the pain
When you're on your own

He's walked the way
Of being misunderstood
He talked the way
To be a friend if he could

He's been in a crowd
And been all alone
He's carried the sorrow
Every heart has borne

He's been on the mountain
In the presence of God
He's been in the valley
Where disease has trodden

He's been in the garden
In the morning to pray
He's been in the darkness
When friends walked away

He's been on the cross
To defeat death and hell
He's been raised from dead
So that heaven can tell

Every tear that you've cried
Has not been unseen
There's a plan for your life
You are part of His dream
Every tear that you've cried

He's working out a way
There's a plan for your life
For your heart's new day

Path In The Sky

Between the earth and sky
We find ourselves
Questioning why
Not knowing where to go
Is the sky
Where we are to be
But we don't know how to go
So walk the earth
Till the day is done
Traveling familiar lands
Then say that you have won
Nothing more can be said
For the path of searching feet
Yet the sun shines on
Showing a land beyond the skies
Away from mortal defeat
One man wise One man a fool
One man looks away
One looks beyond the stars
He sees a cloud like a hand
Reaching to guide
To a distant land

No Matter How Far

No matter how far
He's calling your name
He sees through the hurt
He sees through the pain
He sends out His love
He's calling
He's calling your name

No matter how far
He's calling your name
There's no need to run
There's nothing to gain
So open your heart
Let Him come in
He's calling
He's calling your name

No matter how far
He's calling your name
There's no need to fear
No need to hide
Just wait and see
He will set your heart free
He's calling
He's calling your name

No matter how far
He sees where you are
No matter how far
He sees into your heart
He's calling
He's calling your name

Can you hear Him now
He's closer than before
He keeps calling
Keeps calling
Love keeps calling your name

South Wind Blows

A south wind blows
Down the road of time
Nothing is clear
Light of the sublime
Inside the heart
Mysteries appear
Many paths to take
Though something is clear
Deep inside
A path is revealed
Step by step
A South wind blows
A Spirit wind
Removing the clouds
From my soul
The path through a land
I do not know
It leads to a mountain
A bright cloud surrounds
Lightning, thunder and rain
Call my soul
Till the hungry hearts desire
Is fulfilled

Polished Shoes

Nice Sunday morning
People fill the pews
Time to get started
The parking lot is full

Ushers with polished shoes
Choir starts to sing
Clapping and swaying to the beat
Souls singing Hallelujah
Praise be to the king

One soul takes a run around
Everyone amazed
One soul shakes and falls
Lights are flashing
Machines blowing fog

Jesus stands just outside
A huge angel stands at the door
He turns to Jesus
With a question in his voice
He asks

Why aren't you inside
He said I left long ago
Just came back to check
They still don't know me
They failed every test

This is my last visit
The time has come about
When I return for my remnant
With a trumpet and a shout

Promise

God is a good God
He's a God of mercy and grace
He's a God who's never far away
When we're in a difficult place
Sometimes it seems
We're pushed too far
To the point of no return
But His power and love
Are right by your side
To destroy distress and fear

Cry out to Him
He's with you now
His presence is very near
Cling to His promise of
Forgiveness of sin
Cling to His cross
And His grace
Will flow in
Cling to His Word
Doubt will go
Cling to His shed blood
Healing will flow

Never doubt His promise
Never doubt His Word
Never doubt His touch is near
To the one in faith
He has an open ear

Whirlwind

Got caught up in a whirlwind
Trouble was on every side
Answers seemed to elude me
Nothing could satisfy

Caught up in self-deception
My heart got stolen away
The pain was more than I could stand
Wish I could love and be loved
But it would be only one way

A sick heart is overwhelming
Looking always for a place to rest
Waiting for a relieving word'
An overbearing test

Got caught up in a whirlwind
You would have to be there to know
The hopelessness of a hurting heart
Not a place I recommend you go

Can't move off to an island
Can't live out on the sea
Can't stay up in the mountains
The whirlwind soon will cease

There is a place of solitude
Found only in the Lord
There in His presence
Is the only place to live

Nothing else you can afford

All Along

Been there before
And been back again
Working out life's ways and means
It's an amazing thing
How it all works out
An idea in all of the schemes
It's a wonder things turn out at all
When you consider all the mistakes
Like riding a carousel round and round
Somehow ending up in the right place
Woven into the fabric of the overall plan
There must be a master scheme
What seems like when we have it all
Figured out
We're stuck in the middle of the dream
You must settle inside to do it all right
Inside the conscience will speak
Right when you think you've done it yourself
You remember the times you were weak
Take a step back and look at the times
Things could have turned out all wrong
the unseen hand of the Living God
Was working a plan all along

Mark Of A Man

Eyes of a child look intently on
To the steps of the world
As it builds and forms
Who knows what the design
Of his heart is to be
Who knows what
His future will see
Who knows the unfolding
Of the unseen plan
Who knows
The mark of a man

Eyes of a child look intently on
Men building high towers
As cities are formed
Are they ever satisfied
With their structures of steel
The question remains
What's meaningful and real
What does it come to
Is there a plan
Who really understands
The mark of a man
Eyes of child look intently on
As fortunes are built
And the globe is spanned
Governments rule

Authorities command
As the flower has beauty
But neither toils nor reaps
The child trusts the Father
His soul to keep
If in heaven is stored
This master plan
The child is the father
To the man

The Master said
Let the little children come to me
The Kingdom of God is plain to see
the child's humble heart
Is open and free
If in heaven is ordained
This master plan
Having the heart of a child
Is the mark of a man

Seasons

Sun has set on hopes and dreams
Last light of day fading glory gleams
Leaves have turned
Falling to the earth
Shall eminent death
Bring future birth

Under the sprawling oaks
Knees to the dust
Rivers of tears
Soak the earthly crust
The heart cries out
What's gone so wrong
Shall there be a return
Of the laughter and song

Now only the company of shadows as
The evening air stills and twilight draws near
The dew quietly settles in
On the eve of tomorrow
Can the tears wash away
Yesterday's sorrows

A chilled north wind blows
Hours turn to days
Winter turns the tears to ice
As they stream down the face

Great branches creak
Under the ice and snow
Shall the hibernating heart
Come to understand and know
Lessons unknown
Experiences teaches
Will the heart conceive

Seeds that were sown
Shall the roots shoot forth
And stems rise
With another day
Will it make one wise

The sun melts away the layers of snow
The Earth is warmed
There is a glimmer of hope
The heart watches cautiously
Light breaks the icy skies

Like love broken in young romance
Like leaves in the dust
Dreams lie dormant
The return of trust
Can it revive
Faith failed
Faith tried

Spring sun brings signs of life
Like a maiden awaiting her love
Return from war
Desperate hope fills the span of time

Shall dread of loneliness
Dull the dawn's light
Will there be a smile from heaven
A return of the heart's delight

Ah! Dismayed at life
The future bears change
Wrought in the heart's chambers
Hope exchanges strengths
Dreams begin again

Spirit Wind

Seasons come
And seasons go
Who knows which way
The wind will blow
Seasons of the Spirit's desire
Blows in the heart
Bringing heaven's fire

Have to know
To whom you belong
The heart set free
To sing heaven's song
Glory to the Lamb of God
In His glory we will be
To see His wonderous
Glorious face
And to have a heart set free

Blow Heavenly wind
Set my heart on fire
Blow on Spirit wind of God
Fill me with your desire
Blow sweet wind of God
Blow upon my soul
Blow until
I'm filled with you
Healed, complete, and whole

Blow on
Spirit wind
Blow on
Till I'm free again

About The Author

Author Thomas S. Doland served in the military as an infantryman from 1969 to 1975. During this stint, he learned something of the art of war. He was married in 1969 and had two daughters, one in 1974 and one in 1976. He had a deep experience with God in 1976 which captured his life for missionary service to Africa, India, South America, and Mexico. His love for humanity grew and continues to be his reason to live and breathe. He is directing and financing a school for child slaves in a brickyard in Pakistan, keeping him focused on presenting his writings to challenge and provoke thought outside of common life. Love embraces him and he hopes for love to embrace you to seek and fulfill your purpose.